I0409151

Table Of Contents

What is Email Marketing?..2

Importance of Email Marketing 2

Benefits of Email Marketing 2

Chapter 2: Building an Effective Email List 2

Creating a Target Audience...2

Strategies for Collecting Email Addresses 2

Building a Quality Email List 2

Chapter 3: Crafting Compelling Email Content..................................2

Understanding the Elements of a Successful Email 2

Writing Attention-Grabbing Subject Lines 2

Creating Engaging Email Copy...2

Incorporating Visuals and Multimedia..2

Chapter 4: Designing Effective Email Campaigns..............................2

Planning a Successful Email Campaign 2

Choosing the Right Email Marketing Platform.................................2

Designing Eye-Catching Email Templates 2

Personalizing Email Campaigns...2

Chapter 5: Optimizing Email Deliverability and Open Rates............2

Understanding Email Deliverability...2

Tips for Avoiding Spam Filters..2

Increasing Email Open Rates 2

Testing and Analyzing Email Performance.......................................2

Chapter 6: Automating Email Marketing Campaigns.........................2

Introduction to Email Marketing Automation....................................2

Setting up Automated Email Workflows 2

Nurturing Leads with Drip Campaigns 2

Utilizing Behavioral Triggers...2

Chapter 7: Segmenting and Targeting Email Campaigns 2

Importance of Segmentation in Email Marketing 2

Strategies for Effective Email Segmentation 2

Targeting Specific Customer Segments 2

Personalization Techniques for Higher Conversions 2

Chapter 8: Measuring Email Marketing Success 2

    Key Metrics for Email Marketing 2

    Analyzing Email Campaign Performance 2

    Improving Conversion Rates..2

    A/B Testing for Optimal Results...2

Chapter 9: Enhancing Email Marketing with Advanced Strategies...................2

    Incorporating Social Media into Email Campaigns 2

    Integrating Email with Other Marketing Channels 2

    Leveraging User-Generated Content...2

    Retargeting and Remarketing Techniques.......................................2

Chapter 10: Best Practices and Future Trends in Email Marketing...................2

    Staying Compliant with Email Marketing Regulations 2

    Managing Subscriber Preferences and Opt-outs 2

    Adapting to Evolving Email Marketing Trends 2

    Innovations and Predictions for the Future of Email Marketing...................2

Appendix: 2

    Email Marketing Glossary...2

    Recommended Tools and Resources...2

    Sample Email Templates...2

Chapter 1: Introduction to Email Marketing 1

Chapter 1: Introduction to Email Marketing

What is Email Marketing?

In today's digital age, email marketing has become an indispensable tool for businesses and individuals alike. It offers a powerful way to connect with potential customers, build brand awareness, and drive sales. But what exactly is email marketing, and how can it benefit you?

Email marketing is the practice of sending targeted messages to a group of people via email. These messages can be promotional in nature, such as advertisements or special offers, or they can be informative, providing valuable content and updates. The goal is to engage recipients, nurture relationships, and ultimately, convert them into loyal customers.

For people who want to learn email marketing, understanding its key components is essential. Firstly, building an email list is crucial. This involves collecting email addresses from interested individuals through various channels, such as website sign-up forms, social media campaigns, or events. A quality email list ensures that your messages reach the right audience, increasing the chances of conversion.

Once you have a list, crafting compelling email content is vital. The content should be relevant, personalized, and engaging to capture the reader's attention. This can include informative articles, exclusive discounts, or industry insights. The more value you provide, the more likely your recipients will keep opening your emails and taking the desired action.

To ensure the success of your email marketing campaigns, monitoring and analyzing your results is essential. Email marketing platforms offer valuable metrics, such as open rates, click-through rates, and conversion rates. By tracking these metrics, you can measure the effectiveness of your campaigns and make data-driven decisions to optimize future efforts.

Email marketing offers numerous benefits for businesses. It allows you to reach a large audience instantly, at a fraction of the cost of traditional marketing methods. It also provides a direct line of communication with your customers, fostering loyalty and trust. With the ability to segment your email list based on demographics, interests, or purchasing behavior, you can deliver highly targeted messages that resonate with each recipient.

In conclusion, email marketing is a powerful tool for businesses and individuals looking to connect with their audience, build relationships, and drive sales. By understanding the key components of email marketing, such as list building, content creation, and result analysis, you can harness its potential to achieve your marketing goals. Whether you're a small business owner, a marketer, or an entrepreneur, mastering email marketing is a skill that can propel your success in the digital landscape.

Importance of Email Marketing

Subchapter: Importance of Email Marketing

Welcome to "Mastering Email Marketing: Proven Strategies for Effective Campaigns." In this subchapter, we will explore the importance of email marketing and why it is a crucial tool for anyone interested in reaching their target audience and driving results.

For people who want to learn Email Marketing, understanding its significance is the first step towards harnessing its potential. Email marketing, as a niche, has emerged as a powerful and cost-effective means of communication and promotion. It allows businesses and individuals to directly connect with their target market, build relationships, and drive conversions, all with the click of a button.

One of the primary reasons email marketing is so vital is its incredible reach. With billions of people using email globally, it provides an unparalleled opportunity to connect with a vast audience. Unlike other marketing channels, email marketing allows for personalized, one-on-one communication, making it highly effective in engaging and nurturing leads.

Furthermore, email marketing offers exceptional targeting capabilities. By segmenting your email list based on demographics, interests, or past interactions, you can tailor your messages to specific groups, increasing the chances of conversion. This level of personalization enhances customer experience, builds trust, and boosts brand loyalty.

The ROI (Return on Investment) of email marketing is another compelling reason to prioritize this strategy. With minimal costs compared to traditional marketing methods, such as print or TV, email marketing provides incredible value for money. Studies have consistently shown that email marketing generates a higher ROI compared to other marketing channels, making it an indispensable tool for businesses of all sizes.

Additionally, email marketing allows for precise tracking and analysis. By utilizing email marketing software, you can monitor open rates, click-through rates, and other vital metrics, gaining valuable insights into your campaigns' performance. This data-driven approach enables you to refine your strategies, optimize your content, and ultimately achieve better results.

Lastly, email marketing provides an excellent opportunity for building long-term relationships with your audience. By consistently delivering valuable content, promotions, and updates, you can establish yourself as an authority in your niche and stay top-of-mind for your subscribers. Cultivating this relationship over time can generate repeat business, referrals, and brand ambassadors, contributing to your overall success.

In conclusion, the importance of email marketing cannot be overstated. It is a versatile, cost-effective, and highly targeted marketing tool that allows businesses and individuals to connect with their audience, drive conversions, and achieve measurable results. By mastering the art of email marketing, you will unlock endless possibilities for growth and success in your chosen niche.

Benefits of Email Marketing

In today's digital age, email marketing has become an indispensable tool for businesses and marketers alike. It offers a cost-effective, efficient, and highly targeted way to reach and engage with your audience. If you are someone who wants to learn email marketing, understanding its benefits is crucial for your success. This subchapter will explore the various advantages that email marketing brings to the table.

1. Cost-effective: Email marketing is incredibly cost-effective compared to traditional marketing channels. With minimal expenses, you can design and send personalized emails to a large number of subscribers. This affordability allows businesses of all sizes, from startups to large corporations, to leverage email marketing to their advantage.

2. Increased brand awareness: Consistently sending well-crafted emails to your subscribers helps build brand awareness. By showcasing your products, services, and expertise, you can establish your brand as a trusted authority in your industry. With each email, you reinforce your brand image and increase the chances of your subscribers turning into loyal customers.

3. Enhanced customer engagement: Email marketing enables you to engage with your audience in a more personal and targeted manner. By segmenting your subscribers based on their preferences, demographics, or past interactions, you can send tailored content that resonates with them. This personalized approach fosters stronger relationships and increases customer engagement.

4. Higher conversion rates: When done right, email marketing can yield outstanding conversion rates. By crafting compelling and persuasive emails,

you can encourage recipients to take the desired action, whether it's making a purchase, signing up for a webinar, or downloading an e-book. The ability to track and analyze email metrics allows you to optimize your campaigns and improve conversion rates over time.

5. Improved customer retention: Email marketing is an effective tool for nurturing customer relationships and increasing customer loyalty. By sending regular updates, exclusive offers, and personalized recommendations, you can keep your brand top-of-mind with your subscribers. This consistent communication helps in retaining existing customers and encouraging repeat purchases.

6. Measurable results: One of the key advantages of email marketing is its measurability. Unlike traditional marketing methods, email campaigns provide detailed metrics, allowing you to track open rates, click-through rates, conversion rates, and more. This data provides valuable insights into the success of your campaigns, enabling you to make data-driven decisions and optimize future campaigns.

In conclusion, email marketing offers numerous benefits for businesses and marketers. Its cost-effectiveness, ability to increase brand awareness, enhance customer engagement, improve conversion rates, boost customer retention, and provide measurable results make it an essential component of any successful marketing strategy. By mastering the art of email marketing, you can unlock its immense potential and harness its power to grow your business and achieve your marketing goals.

Chapter 2: Building an Effective Email List

Creating a Target Audience

In the world of email marketing, one of the most crucial steps in developing an effective campaign is identifying and understanding your target audience. Without a clear understanding of who you are trying to reach and engage with, your efforts may fall flat and fail to produce the desired results.

To begin creating a target audience, it is essential to conduct thorough research and gather relevant data. This can be done through various methods, such as surveys, interviews, and analyzing existing customer data. The goal is to gain insights into your potential customers' demographics, interests, preferences, and behaviors.

Demographics play a significant role in understanding your target audience. Factors such as age, gender, location, and income level can help you tailor your email marketing campaigns to resonate with specific groups. For example, if you are promoting a fashion brand targeting young women, your emails should reflect their preferences and showcase products that align with their style and interests.

Understanding your audience's interests and preferences is equally vital. This can be achieved by analyzing their online activities, social media interactions, and previous purchases. By knowing what your audience is passionate about and what motivates them, you can create personalized and engaging email content that speaks directly to their needs and desires.

Behavioral data is another valuable resource when creating a target audience. By tracking your audience's actions and engagement with your emails, you can gain insights into their buying patterns, browsing habits, and level of interaction. This information can help you segment your audience and send targeted emails based on their behaviors, increasing the likelihood of conversions.

Once you have gathered and analyzed all the necessary data, it is time to create buyer personas. These fictional representations of your ideal customers will guide your email marketing strategy. A buyer persona includes details about your audience's demographics, interests, pain points, and goals. By referring to these personas, you can tailor your email campaigns to address their specific needs and desires, creating a deeper connection and driving engagement.

In conclusion, creating a target audience is a vital step in mastering email marketing. By understanding the demographics, interests, and behaviors of your potential customers, you can develop personalized and impactful email campaigns that resonate with your audience. Investing time and effort into this process will significantly increase your chances of success in the competitive world of email marketing.

Strategies for Collecting Email Addresses

Subchapter: Strategies for Collecting Email Addresses

In the world of email marketing, building a strong and engaged subscriber list is crucial for the success of your campaigns. Being able to collect email addresses effectively is the foundation upon which your email marketing strategy is built. In this subchapter, we will explore some proven strategies for collecting email addresses that will help you grow your subscriber list and enhance the effectiveness of your email marketing campaigns.

1. Offer Valuable Content: One of the most effective ways to entice people to share their email addresses is by offering valuable content in exchange. Create high-quality lead magnets such as ebooks, whitepapers, or exclusive guides that align with your target audience's interests. Promote these lead magnets on your website, blog, or social media platforms to encourage visitors to subscribe to your email list.

2. Opt-in Forms and Pop-ups: Opt-in forms and pop-ups strategically placed on your website can significantly boost your email subscription rate. Use compelling copy and design to grab visitors' attention and clearly communicate the value they will receive by subscribing. Experiment with different placements and timing options to find what works best for your audience.

3. Landing Pages: Dedicated landing pages can be powerful tools for collecting email addresses. Create landing pages with persuasive copy and visually appealing designs that highlight the benefits of subscribing to your email list. Drive traffic to these pages through social media ads, guest blogging, or email campaigns to capture more leads.

4. Contests and Giveaways: People love the chance to win something. Organize contests or giveaways that require participants to submit their email addresses for entry. Ensure that the prize aligns with your target audience's interests, and promote the contest on your website, social media, and other relevant platforms to maximize participation.

5. Social Media Lead Generation: Leverage the power of social media to collect email addresses. Use lead generation ads on platforms like Facebook, Instagram, or LinkedIn to capture email addresses directly. Additionally, drive traffic to your landing pages or opt-in forms through engaging social media posts, encouraging your followers to subscribe.

6. Co-Marketing and Partnerships: Collaborate with influencers, complementary brands, or industry experts to reach a wider audience and collect email addresses. Offer co-branded content, webinars, or exclusive discounts that require participants to subscribe to your email list. This strategy not only helps in collecting more email addresses but also strengthens your brand's credibility.

Remember, building an email list is an ongoing process. Continuously monitor and analyze the effectiveness of your strategies, and be open to experimenting with new approaches. By implementing these proven strategies for collecting email addresses, you will be well on your way to mastering email marketing and achieving successful campaigns.

Building a Quality Email List

In the world of email marketing, success hinges on having a quality email list. Your list is the foundation upon which you will build effective campaigns and connect with your target audience. In this subchapter, we will explore strategies and best practices for building a high-quality email list that will drive engagement and conversions.

1. Define your target audience: Before you start building your email list, it's crucial to clearly define your target audience. Understand their demographics, interests, and pain points. This will help you tailor your campaigns and ensure that the subscribers you attract are relevant to your business.

2. Create compelling opt-in offers: To entice visitors to join your email list, you need to provide them with valuable incentives. This could be a free e-book, a discount code, or exclusive access to premium content. Make sure your opt-in offers align with your target audience's needs and desires.

3. Optimize your website for sign-ups: Place sign-up forms strategically on your website to maximize conversions. Use eye-catching calls-to-action (CTAs) and ensure that the form is easy to fill out. Offer multiple opportunities for visitors to join your list, such as pop-ups, sidebar forms, or exit-intent pop-ups.

4. Leverage social media: Promote your email list on social media platforms to reach a wider audience. Encourage your followers to subscribe by highlighting the benefits they will receive. Run contests or giveaways exclusively for subscribers to boost sign-ups.

5. Use landing pages: Create dedicated landing pages that focus solely on capturing email addresses. These pages should be designed to convert visitors into subscribers. Keep the form simple and remove any distractions that might hinder conversions.

6. Implement double opt-in: Double opt-in is a process that requires subscribers to confirm their email address after signing up. This helps ensure that the email addresses on your list are valid and engaged. It also helps you comply with anti-spam regulations.

7. Segment your list: As your email list grows, it's crucial to segment your subscribers based on their interests and behaviors. This allows you to send targeted and relevant content, resulting in higher engagement and conversion rates.

Remember, building a quality email list is an ongoing process. Regularly evaluate your strategies, monitor your metrics, and make adjustments as needed. By focusing on attracting engaged subscribers who align with your target audience, you will create a foundation for successful email marketing campaigns.

Chapter 3: Crafting Compelling Email Content

Understanding the Elements of a Successful Email

In the world of digital marketing, email remains one of the most effective and popular communication channels. Email marketing allows businesses to reach out to their target audience, build relationships, and drive conversions. However, crafting a successful email campaign requires a deep understanding of the key elements that make up an impactful email. In this subchapter, we will explore these elements and provide valuable insights on how to create effective emails that yield impressive results.

Subject Line: The subject line is the first thing recipients see in their inbox. It is crucial to create a subject line that grabs attention, sparks curiosity, and entices recipients to open the email. We will discuss various strategies and techniques to craft compelling subject lines that increase open rates.

Content: The content of your email should be engaging, relevant, and personalized. We will explore how to structure your email, use persuasive language, and create compelling calls-to-action. Additionally, we will delve into the power of storytelling and how it can be used to captivate readers and inspire action.

Design and Layout: A visually appealing email can significantly impact the recipient's engagement. We will discuss the importance of using eye-catching designs, branding elements, and consistent layout across different devices and email clients. We will also cover the significance of mobile-responsive designs, as a large number of people now access their emails on mobile devices.

Personalization and Segmentation: Personalization is key to creating a successful email campaign. We will delve into the importance of segmenting your email list based on various criteria such as demographics, past behavior, and purchase history. We will also explore how to personalize your emails to make them more relevant and engaging for each recipient.

Testing and Optimization: To ensure the success of your email campaigns, it is essential to test and optimize your emails continuously. We will discuss various testing strategies, including A/B testing, and how to analyze the results to improve your future campaigns. Additionally, we will explore the importance of tracking key metrics such as open rates, click-through rates, and conversion rates.

By understanding and implementing these key elements of a successful email, you will be well-equipped to create effective email campaigns that engage your audience, drive conversions, and ultimately achieve your marketing goals.

Writing Attention-Grabbing Subject Lines

In the world of email marketing, subject lines are the gateways to your audience's attention. They are the first impression, the teaser, and the deciding factor on whether your email gets opened or sent straight to the trash bin. It's no wonder that crafting attention-grabbing subject lines is a crucial skill for anyone looking to excel in email marketing.

To truly master the art of writing subject lines that capture attention, it's important to understand the psychology behind what makes people click. One of the key elements is curiosity. Humans are naturally curious creatures, and a subject line that piques their curiosity is more likely to make them click. For example, "Unlock the Secrets to Doubling Your Sales" or "Discover the Hidden Strategies of Successful Email Marketers" are subject lines that tap into people's desire to learn something new and valuable.

Another effective technique is personalization. People love to feel special and addressed directly. By including the recipient's name or using language that speaks directly to their needs and desires, you can create a sense of personal connection that entices them to open the email. For instance, "John, Boost Your Email Marketing ROI with These Proven Tactics" or "Attention Small Business Owners: Get More Customers with Email Marketing" are subject lines that feel tailored specifically to the recipient.

Urgency is also a powerful motivator. By creating a sense of urgency in your subject lines, you can encourage your audience to take immediate action. Limited-time offers, exclusive deals, or time-sensitive information can all be used to create a sense of urgency. For example, "Last Chance: 50% Off Ends Tonight!" or "Important Updates: Don't Miss Out on the Latest Email Marketing Trends" are subject lines that trigger a fear of missing out and prompt immediate action.

Lastly, it's important to keep your subject lines concise and to the point. In today's fast-paced digital world, people have short attention spans and are bombarded with numerous emails every day. A subject line that is too long or vague will likely be skimmed over or ignored entirely. Instead, aim for subject lines that are clear, intriguing, and can be understood at a glance.

In conclusion, writing attention-grabbing subject lines is an essential skill for every email marketer. By tapping into curiosity, personalization, urgency, and keeping your subject lines concise, you can increase open rates, engage your audience, and drive the success of your email marketing campaigns.

Creating Engaging Email Copy

In the digital age, where our inboxes are flooded with countless emails, it is crucial for email marketers to create engaging email copy that captivates their audience's attention. Crafting compelling email content is the key to standing out in a cluttered inbox and driving successful email marketing campaigns. In this subchapter, we will explore proven strategies and techniques to help you master the art of creating engaging email copy.

1. Know Your Audience: Understanding your target audience is essential when it comes to crafting effective email copy. Research your audience's preferences, needs, and pain points to personalize your message and make it relevant to their interests. By tailoring your content to their specific needs, you will increase engagement and improve the chances of conversion.

2. Grab Attention with a Strong Subject Line: The subject line is the first impression your email makes, so it needs to be attention-grabbing. Use action-oriented language, create a sense of urgency, or ask intriguing questions to entice your audience to open the email. A compelling subject line sets the tone for the rest of the email and increases the chances of it being read.

3. Craft Clear and Concise Content: People have limited time and attention spans, so it's crucial to keep your email copy clear and concise. Use short paragraphs, bullet points, and subheadings to make your content scannable. Focus on delivering a clear message and avoid overwhelming your readers with excessive information. Use persuasive language to connect with your audience and evoke emotion.

4. Personalize Your Emails: Personalization is a powerful tool in email marketing. Address your recipients by their names and segment your audience based on their preferences or past interactions. Tailoring your email copy to each segment allows you to provide more relevant and valuable content, leading to higher engagement rates.

5. Use Compelling Visuals: Incorporating visually appealing elements, such as images, videos, or GIFs, can significantly enhance the impact of your email copy. Visuals not only make your emails more engaging but also help convey your message more effectively. Ensure your visuals are on-brand and support the overall message of your email.

6. Include a Strong Call-to-Action: Every email should have a clear and compelling call-to-action (CTA) that prompts readers to take the desired action. Use action verbs, create a sense of urgency, and make your CTA stand

out visually. A well-designed and strategically placed CTA can significantly increase conversions.

By implementing these strategies and techniques, you will be able to create email copy that engages your audience, drives conversions, and ultimately achieves your email marketing goals. Remember to continuously test and optimize your email copy based on the feedback and analytics you receive. Mastering the art of creating engaging email copy is a continuous process, and with practice, you will become a highly effective email marketer.

Incorporating Visuals and Multimedia

In today's digital world, where attention spans are shorter than ever, incorporating visuals and multimedia into your email marketing campaigns is crucial to capturing your audience's attention and driving engagement. Visual content not only enhances the overall aesthetics of your emails, but it also helps convey your message more effectively. In this subchapter, we will explore the various ways you can leverage visuals and multimedia to create compelling email marketing campaigns that yield exceptional results.

First and foremost, let's discuss the power of images. Including relevant and eye-catching images in your emails can significantly boost the click-through rates and conversion rates of your campaigns. Whether it's product images, infographics, or enticing visuals that highlight your services, pictures can instantly grab your subscribers' attention and make your message more memorable. Moreover, images can help break up text-heavy emails, making them more digestible and visually appealing.

Additionally, videos have become an incredibly popular form of content consumption. By incorporating videos into your email marketing strategy, you can effectively communicate your brand's story, showcase product demonstrations, or even provide valuable tutorials to your subscribers. Videos not only foster a more personal connection with your audience but also increase the time spent engaging with your emails. Remember to optimize your videos for mobile devices, as a significant portion of email opens occur on smartphones and tablets.

Infographics, charts, and interactive elements are other powerful visual tools that can transform your emails into engaging experiences. These visual elements help simplify complex information and statistics, making it easier for your subscribers to understand and retain the key points you're trying to convey. Furthermore, interactive elements like quizzes, surveys, or GIFs can add an element of fun and interactivity, encouraging your audience to actively participate and share your emails with others.

When incorporating visuals and multimedia into your email marketing campaigns, it's essential to strike a balance between aesthetics and performance. While visually appealing emails can capture attention, it's crucial to ensure that they load quickly and are optimized for different email clients and devices. Additionally, always provide alternative text descriptions for images and videos, catering to subscribers who may have visual impairments or those who have email clients that don't display visuals by default.

Incorporating visuals and multimedia into your email marketing campaigns can significantly enhance your overall strategy, leading to increased engagement, conversions, and brand loyalty. By experimenting with different types of visuals, testing their performance, and continuously refining your approach, you can master the art of leveraging visual content to create compelling and effective email marketing campaigns.

Chapter 4: Designing Effective Email Campaigns

Planning a Successful Email Campaign

Email marketing has become an indispensable tool for businesses and marketers looking to connect with their target audience effectively. To make the most of this powerful strategy, careful planning is essential. This subchapter on "Planning a Successful Email Campaign" aims to provide a comprehensive guide to help individuals and businesses create effective email campaigns that yield tangible results.

1. Defining Objectives: Before diving into the campaign, it is crucial to define clear objectives. Whether it is increasing sales, generating leads, or building brand awareness, having a clear goal in mind will help shape the entire campaign strategy.

2. Identifying Target Audience: Understanding your target audience is key to crafting personalized and relevant email content. By analyzing demographics, interests, and behavior, you can segment your email list to ensure that your messages reach the right people at the right time.

3. Creating Engaging Content: Crafting compelling content is the backbone of any successful email campaign. From catchy subject lines to captivating copy, each element should be carefully designed to grab the reader's attention and encourage them to take action.

4. Designing Responsive Templates: With the increasing use of mobile devices, it is imperative to create responsive email templates that adapt to different screen sizes. A visually appealing and user-friendly design will enhance the overall user experience and increase the chances of conversions.

5. Optimizing for Deliverability: Ensuring that your emails land in the recipients' inbox rather than the spam folder is crucial for a successful campaign. Implementing best practices such as having a clean email list, avoiding spam trigger words, and segmenting your audience can significantly improve deliverability rates.

6. Testing and Analyzing: A/B testing different elements of your email campaign, such as subject lines, call-to-action buttons, and content, can provide valuable insights into what resonates best with your audience. Regularly analyzing key metrics like open rates, click-through rates, and conversions will help refine your strategy and achieve better results over time.

7. Automation and Personalization: Leveraging automation tools and personalization techniques can significantly enhance the effectiveness of your email campaigns. By sending targeted and personalized messages based on user behavior and preferences, you can establish stronger connections with your subscribers and drive higher engagement.

In conclusion, planning a successful email campaign requires a strategic approach and attention to detail. By defining clear objectives, understanding your target audience, creating engaging content, optimizing for deliverability, and leveraging automation and personalization, you can master the art of email marketing and achieve your desired outcomes. This subchapter provides the necessary guidance and best practices for those looking to excel in the realm of email marketing.

Choosing the Right Email Marketing Platform

As email marketing continues to be one of the most effective forms of digital marketing, it is crucial to select the right email marketing platform that aligns with your goals and objectives. With numerous platforms available in the market, it can be overwhelming to make the right choice. In this subchapter, we will guide you through the process of selecting the perfect email marketing platform for your needs.

When choosing an email marketing platform, it is essential to consider factors such as user-friendliness, automation capabilities, integration options, pricing, and customer support. These factors will help you narrow down your options and ensure that the platform you choose meets your specific requirements.

First and foremost, consider the platform's user-friendliness. A user-friendly interface will save you time and make it easier to navigate through the platform's features. Look for drag-and-drop editors, pre-designed templates, and customizable options that allow you to create visually appealing and engaging emails without the need for coding skills.

Automation is another crucial aspect to consider. A good email marketing platform should offer robust automation capabilities, allowing you to set up automated campaigns based on triggers, such as subscriber behavior, purchase history, or specific events. Automation will help you save time, streamline your campaigns, and deliver personalized and timely content to your subscribers.

Integration options are vital for seamless workflow. Ensure that the platform integrates with other tools you use, such as customer relationship management (CRM) systems, e-commerce platforms, or analytics tools. Integration will enable you to leverage data from various sources to create targeted and effective email campaigns.

Pricing is also an important consideration. While some email marketing platforms offer free plans or low-cost options for beginners, they may have limitations in terms of features or subscriber numbers. Evaluate your budget and choose a platform that aligns with your financial capabilities while providing the necessary features for your campaigns. Additionally, consider the scalability of the platform; as your email list grows, you might need to upgrade to a higher plan.

Lastly, customer support is crucial, especially for beginners. Look for platforms that provide comprehensive customer support, including live chat, email, or phone support. Having access to prompt assistance can save you valuable time and help you resolve any technical issues or concerns efficiently.

By carefully considering these factors, you can confidently choose the right email marketing platform that suits your needs, ensuring the success and effectiveness of your email campaigns. Remember, the right platform will empower you to engage with your subscribers, increase conversions, and ultimately achieve your email marketing goals.

Here's a step-by-step guide to help you set up automated emails using Mailchimp:

Step 1: Create a Mailchimp Account Go to the Mailchimp website (www.mailchimp.com) and sign up for a new account if you don't already have one. Follow the prompts to create your account and verify your email address.

Step 2: Set Up Your List Log in to your Mailchimp account. Click on the "Audience" tab in the top navigation menu. Click on "Audience dashboard." Click the "Create Audience" button and follow the prompts to set up your email list.

Step 3: Create an Automation Workflow After setting up your list, click on the "Automations" tab in the top navigation menu. Click on the "Create" button to start creating a new automation workflow.

Step 4: Choose an Automation Type Select the type of automation you want to create. Common options include "Welcome new subscribers," "E-commerce customer," "Abandoned cart," etc. Choose the one that fits your needs.

Step 5: Configure Trigger Configure the trigger that will start the automation. For example, if you're setting up a "Welcome" automation, the trigger could be when someone subscribes to your list. Follow the prompts to set up the trigger conditions and options.

Step 6: Design Your Email Design the email that you want to send as part of the automation. You can use Mailchimp's drag-and-drop email editor to customize the email's content and appearance. Add relevant content, images, links, and personalization.

Step 7: Schedule and Settings Configure the schedule for your automated email. You can choose to send the email immediately after the trigger or set a delay. Set any additional settings such as segmenting your audience, choosing sending days, and time.

Step 8: Review and Test Review your automation workflow to ensure that all settings, triggers, and emails are configured correctly. Send a test email to yourself to see how it looks and ensure that everything is working as expected.

Step 9: Activate Automation Once you're satisfied with your automated email setup, click the "Activate" button to make it live. Your automated emails will now be sent out according to the trigger and schedule you've set up.

Step 10: Monitor and Optimize Regularly monitor the performance of your automated emails through the Mailchimp dashboard. Use the analytics and insights provided by Mailchimp to optimize your automated email campaigns over time.

That's it! You've successfully set up automated emails using Mailchimp. Remember that Mailchimp's interface might evolve, so make sure to refer to their official documentation or support resources if you encounter any specific changes or issues during the setup process.

Other Email Marketing Tools:

Constant Contact

HubSpot Email Marketing

GetResponse

AWeber

ConvertKit

Campaign Monitor

ActiveCampaign

SendinBlue

MailerLite

Designing Eye-Catching Email Templates

When it comes to email marketing, one of the most crucial aspects is creating eye-catching email templates that grab the attention of your audience. In this subchapter, we will explore proven strategies and techniques to help you design visually appealing emails that convert.

1. Know Your Audience: Before diving into the design process, it's essential to understand your target audience. Consider their preferences, demographics, and interests. This knowledge will enable you to create email templates that resonate with your audience and increase engagement.

2. Keep it Simple: In the world of email marketing, simplicity is key. Ensure that your email templates have a clean layout, easy-to-read fonts, and a logical flow. Avoid overwhelming your recipients with excessive images, text, or

flashy graphics. A clutter-free design will make your message more digestible and increase the chances of conversion.

3. Consistent Branding: Consistency is crucial in building brand recognition. Incorporate your brand elements such as logo, colors, and typography into your email templates. This will help your audience identify and connect with your brand, even in their inbox.

4. Mobile-Friendly Design: With the rise of smartphones, it is essential to optimize your email templates for mobile devices. Ensure that your templates are responsive and adapt seamlessly to different screen sizes. A mobile-friendly design will enhance the user experience and prevent recipients from deleting or ignoring your emails.

5. Visual Hierarchy: Use visual hierarchy techniques to guide your reader's attention to the most important elements of your email. Use larger fonts, bold headings, and strategic placement of images and buttons to draw attention to your call-to-action (CTA). This will encourage recipients to take the desired action.

6. Personalization: Personalization is a powerful tool in email marketing. Tailor your email templates to include the recipient's name or other relevant details. This will create a sense of connection and increase the chances of engagement and conversions.

7. A/B Testing: Don't be afraid to experiment with different email templates. Conduct A/B testing to determine which designs perform better and generate higher engagement rates. Test different elements such as subject lines, colors, layouts, and CTAs to optimize your email templates.

In conclusion, designing eye-catching email templates is a crucial component of successful email marketing campaigns. By understanding your audience, keeping the design simple yet visually appealing, and optimizing for mobile devices, you can create emails that capture attention and drive conversions.

Incorporate consistent branding, utilize visual hierarchy techniques, personalize your emails, and conduct A/B testing to continuously improve your email templates and achieve maximum results in your email marketing efforts.

Personalizing Email Campaigns

In the fast-paced digital world, email marketing remains a powerful tool for businesses to reach their target audience effectively. However, with the increasing number of emails flooding individuals' inboxes, it is crucial to stand out from the crowd and capture the attention of your recipients. This is where personalization comes into play.

Personalizing email campaigns is an essential strategy that helps marketers connect with their audience on a deeper level and foster meaningful relationships. By tailoring your messages to individual recipients, you can create a more personalized experience that resonates with their interests and needs.

To begin personalizing your email campaigns, it is vital to gather relevant data about your subscribers. This can include basic information such as name, location, and gender, as well as more detailed data like purchase history and browsing behavior. By segmenting your audience based on this data, you can create targeted campaigns that cater to specific interests and preferences.

One effective way to personalize your emails is by addressing each recipient by their name in the subject line or the opening line of the email. This simple touch can make your messages feel more personal and engaging. Additionally, using dynamic content allows you to showcase different products or offers based on the recipient's past behavior or preferences, increasing the chances of conversion.

Beyond personalization based on demographic or behavioral data, it is also important to consider the timing and frequency of your email campaigns.

Understanding your audience's habits and preferences can help you send emails at the most opportune moments, ensuring that your messages are received and read by the right people.

Furthermore, personalizing email campaigns goes beyond just the content. Paying attention to the design and layout of your emails can also make a significant impact. Use visually appealing templates and ensure that your emails are mobile-friendly to provide a seamless experience across different devices.

Remember, personalization is not just a one-time effort. Continuously tracking and analyzing data can help you refine your personalization strategies and optimize your email campaigns for better results. Regularly test different elements, such as subject lines, CTAs, and personalization techniques, to determine what resonates best with your audience.

In conclusion, personalizing email campaigns is a powerful technique that can help you cut through the noise and engage your audience effectively. By leveraging data and employing targeted strategies, you can create personalized experiences that build trust, loyalty, and drive conversions. Stay tuned for the next chapter, where we will delve deeper into advanced personalization techniques and best practices for mastering email marketing.

Chapter 5: Optimizing Email Deliverability and Open Rates

Understanding Email Deliverability

Email deliverability is a critical aspect of email marketing that directly affects the success of your campaigns. In this subchapter, we will delve into the intricacies of email deliverability and provide you with valuable insights to ensure your messages reach the intended recipients' inboxes.

When it comes to email marketing, your ultimate goal is to have your emails successfully delivered and engaged with by your target audience. However, several factors can impact your email deliverability, including spam filters, sender reputation, and content quality.

Spam filters play a significant role in determining whether your emails end up in the inbox or spam folder. These filters analyze various aspects of your email, such as subject lines, sender information, and content, to determine its legitimacy. To ensure your emails bypass spam filters, it is essential to follow best practices, such as avoiding spam trigger words, using a reputable email service provider, and personalizing your emails.

Sender reputation is another crucial factor influencing your email deliverability. Internet service providers (ISPs) evaluate the reputation of the sender's IP address and domain to determine the credibility of your emails. Maintaining a positive sender reputation involves adhering to email marketing guidelines, keeping complaint rates low, and regularly monitoring deliverability metrics.

Content quality plays a vital role in email deliverability as well. ISPs assess the email's content for relevance, engagement, and value to the recipient. Crafting compelling subject lines, providing valuable content, and avoiding excessive promotional language can significantly improve your chances of reaching the inbox.

Furthermore, ensuring that your email list is clean and regularly updated is crucial for optimal deliverability. Removing inactive or unengaged subscribers from your list can improve engagement rates and prevent your emails from being flagged as spam.

Monitoring and analyzing deliverability metrics is essential to optimize your email marketing campaigns. Metrics like open rates, click-through rates, bounce rates, and spam complaints provide valuable insights into the effectiveness of your email strategy. Regularly reviewing these metrics and making necessary adjustments will help you improve your email deliverability over time.

In conclusion, understanding email deliverability is essential for anyone venturing into email marketing. By following best practices, maintaining a positive sender reputation, crafting quality content, and monitoring deliverability metrics, you can ensure that your emails reach the intended recipients' inboxes and achieve maximum engagement.

Tips for Avoiding Spam Filters

In the ever-evolving world of email marketing, one of the biggest challenges marketers face is ensuring their messages reach the intended recipients' inboxes. With the prevalence of spam filters, it has become increasingly important to understand how to avoid being flagged as spam and optimize the deliverability of your email campaigns. Here are some valuable tips to help you navigate this obstacle and ensure your messages are reaching your audience.

1. Build a quality email list: Start by building an email list composed of engaged subscribers who have willingly opted-in to receive your messages. Avoid purchasing or renting email lists, as these often contain outdated or

inactive addresses, which can increase the chances of your emails being marked as spam.

2. Use a reputable email service provider: Partnering with a reliable email service provider (ESP) is essential. Reputable ESPs have established relationships with ISPs (Internet Service Providers) and maintain good sender reputations, increasing the chances of your emails being delivered to the inbox.

3. Authenticate your emails: Implement authentication protocols such as SPF (Sender Policy Framework) and DKIM (DomainKeys Identified Mail) to verify your identity and improve your sender reputation. These protocols help ISPs recognize your emails as legitimate, reducing the likelihood of them being flagged as spam.

4. Craft relevant and engaging content: Ensure your emails provide value to your subscribers and align with their expectations. Tailor your content to their interests and preferences, and avoid using deceptive subject lines or misleading information. By delivering valuable content consistently, you can build trust and reduce the chances of your emails being marked as spam.

5. Monitor your sender reputation: Regularly monitor your sender reputation using tools like SenderScore or BarracudaCentral. These tools provide insights into your deliverability rates and help identify potential issues that could harm your sender reputation.

6. Test your emails before sending: Before launching a campaign, test your emails using spam filter testing tools. These tools evaluate your emails for potential spam triggers and provide recommendations for improvement. By addressing any issues beforehand, you can increase the chances of your emails reaching the inbox.

7. Implement a double opt-in process: Use a double opt-in process to confirm subscribers' intentions and ensure the accuracy of their email addresses. This

helps maintain a clean and engaged email list, reducing the risk of your emails being marked as spam.

By following these tips, you can improve your email deliverability and avoid falling victim to spam filters. Remember, building a good sender reputation, providing valuable content, and adhering to email marketing best practices are key to achieving successful email campaigns that reach your audience's inboxes.

Increasing Email Open Rates

In the world of email marketing, the success of your campaigns heavily relies on one crucial metric: the open rate. After all, if your subscribers are not opening your emails, your carefully crafted content and compelling offers will go unnoticed. So how can you increase your email open rates and capture the attention of your audience? Let's dive into some proven strategies that will help you master this essential aspect of email marketing.

1. Craft Irresistible Subject Lines: The subject line is the first thing your subscribers see in their inbox, and it plays a crucial role in determining whether or not they will open your email. Create subject lines that are concise, intriguing, and personalized to grab their attention and entice them to click.

2. Segment Your Email List: Sending the same email to your entire list may not yield the best results. By segmenting your email list based on demographics, interests, or past interactions, you can tailor your messages to specific audience segments, making them more relevant and increasing the chances of higher open rates.

3. Personalize Your Emails: People are more likely to open and engage with emails that feel personalized. Use your subscriber's name in the subject line or greeting, and leverage any available data to deliver targeted and relevant content that resonates with their specific needs or preferences.

4. Optimize Email Timing: Timing is everything when it comes to email marketing. Experiment with different send times and days of the week to identify when your audience is most likely to open and engage with your emails. Consider the time zones of your subscribers to ensure your messages reach them at the most opportune moments.

5. A/B Test Your Emails: Don't leave your email open rates to chance. Conduct A/B tests to compare different email elements such as subject lines, preview text, or even email design. Analyze the results to identify which variations generate higher open rates and apply those insights to future campaigns.

6. Cleanse Your Email List: Over time, your email list may accumulate inactive or disengaged subscribers who no longer open your emails. Regularly clean your list by removing these contacts to maintain a healthy open rate and improve the overall effectiveness of your email campaigns.

By implementing these strategies, you can significantly increase your email open rates, ensuring that your carefully crafted content reaches and engages with your target audience. Remember, email marketing is an ever-evolving field, so always stay updated on the latest trends and best practices to stay ahead of the competition and achieve long-term success.

Testing and Analyzing Email Performance

In the world of email marketing, one of the most crucial steps for achieving success is testing and analyzing the performance of your campaigns. Without proper testing and analysis, it becomes nearly impossible to determine what works and what doesn't. In this subchapter, we will delve into the importance of testing and analyzing email performance and provide you with essential strategies to optimize your campaigns.

Testing is the backbone of any successful email marketing campaign. It allows you to experiment with different elements of your emails, such as subject lines, copy, design, and calls to action, to determine which variations resonate the most with your audience. By conducting A/B testing, where you send two different versions of an email to a select group of subscribers and measure their response, you can gain valuable insights into what drives engagement and conversion.

There are various elements you can test within your emails. Subject lines, for example, play a crucial role in enticing recipients to open your emails. Test different subject lines to see which ones generate higher open rates. Additionally, test different email designs, including color schemes, layouts, and images, to gauge which resonate best with your audience.

Analyzing email performance is equally important as testing. By closely monitoring key metrics such as open rates, click-through rates, conversion rates, and unsubscribe rates, you can gauge the effectiveness of your campaigns and make data-driven decisions to improve future campaigns. Analyzing these metrics allows you to identify trends, understand user behavior, and optimize your email marketing strategy accordingly.

Furthermore, segmentation and personalization are vital aspects of email marketing. By segmenting your email list based on various criteria such as demographics, interests, or past purchase behavior, you can tailor your emails to specific groups of subscribers, increasing the chances of engagement and conversion. Analyzing the performance of segmented campaigns will help you understand which segments yield the best results and enable you to refine your targeting strategy.

In conclusion, testing and analyzing email performance is essential for mastering email marketing. By conducting thorough testing, you can optimize various elements of your emails to maximize engagement and conversion. Equally important is analyzing key metrics to gain insights into your audience's behavior and preferences. Through continuous testing and analysis, you can refine your email marketing strategy, improve campaign performance, and achieve desired results.

Chapter 6: Automating Email Marketing Campaigns

Introduction to Email Marketing Automation

Email marketing automation is a powerful tool that has revolutionized the way businesses communicate with their customers. In today's digital age, email remains one of the most effective and cost-efficient marketing channels. It allows businesses to connect with their target audience on a personal level, delivering relevant and timely messages that drive engagement, conversions, and customer loyalty.

This subchapter aims to provide an introduction to email marketing automation for individuals who want to learn the ins and outs of this dynamic field. Whether you are a small business owner, a marketer, or an aspiring email marketing professional, this chapter will equip you with the knowledge and strategies needed to harness the full potential of email marketing automation.

In the first section, we will delve into the basics of email marketing, explaining what it is and why it is crucial for businesses of all sizes. We will explore the various benefits of email marketing, such as its high return on investment, scalability, and ability to reach a wide audience. Understanding the foundational principles of email marketing will set the stage for diving into the world of automation.

Next, we will introduce the concept of email marketing automation and its significance in today's fast-paced business environment. Email automation involves using software and tools to streamline and personalize email campaigns, making them more efficient and effective. We will discuss the key features and capabilities of email marketing automation platforms, as well as the various types of automated email campaigns that businesses can implement.

Furthermore, this subchapter will explore the essential elements of successful email marketing automation. We will discuss the importance of building a quality email list, segmenting your audience, and creating engaging content that resonates with your subscribers. Additionally, we will explore the role of analytics and tracking in email marketing automation, allowing businesses to measure and optimize their campaigns for maximum results.

Throughout this subchapter, we will provide practical tips, best practices, and real-world examples to illustrate the power and potential of email marketing automation. By the end of this chapter, you will have a solid foundation in email marketing automation and be well-equipped to develop and execute effective email campaigns that drive results.

Whether you are new to email marketing or looking to enhance your skills, this subchapter will empower you to take your email marketing efforts to the next level. Get ready to master email marketing automation and unlock the full potential of this indispensable marketing channel.

Setting up Automated Email Workflows

In the fast-paced world of email marketing, automation has become a game-changer. By setting up automated email workflows, you can streamline your campaigns, save time, and increase efficiency. In this subchapter, we will delve into the intricacies of setting up automated email workflows, providing you with proven strategies for effective campaigns.

Automated email workflows are a series of pre-defined emails that are triggered based on specific actions or events. These workflows enable you to deliver personalized and timely content to your subscribers, enhancing their engagement and ultimately driving conversions.

The first step in setting up automated email workflows is to identify the goals of your campaign. Are you aiming to nurture leads, onboard new customers, or re-engage inactive subscribers? Once you have a clear objective in mind, you can start designing your workflow.

Segmentation plays a crucial role in successful email marketing. By categorizing your subscribers based on their interests, preferences, or behavior, you can tailor your automated workflows accordingly. This allows you to create targeted, relevant content that resonates with your audience.

Next, you need to determine the triggers that will initiate your automated workflows. Triggers can include actions such as subscribing to your newsletter, abandoning a cart, or completing a purchase. By understanding your subscribers' actions, you can send them the right message at the right time.

Crafting compelling and engaging email content is essential for the success of your automated workflows. Each email in the workflow should have a clear purpose and a strong call-to-action. Whether it's providing valuable information, offering a discount, or inviting subscribers to an event, your emails should deliver value and drive the desired action.

Testing and optimization are essential components of any email marketing campaign. By analyzing the performance of your automated workflows, you can identify areas for improvement and make data-driven decisions. A/B testing different elements such as subject lines, CTAs, and email layouts can help you refine your workflows and achieve better results.

In conclusion, setting up automated email workflows is a powerful strategy for email marketers. By leveraging the right triggers, segmentation, and content, you can deliver personalized, timely messages that resonate with your audience. With careful planning, testing, and optimization, you can master the art of automated email workflows and drive effective campaigns that yield impressive results.

Nurturing Leads with Drip Campaigns

In the world of email marketing, nurturing leads is crucial for building strong relationships with potential customers. One effective strategy to accomplish this is through the use of drip campaigns. This subchapter will delve into the concept of drip campaigns and how they can be leveraged to maximize your email marketing efforts.

Drip campaigns involve sending a series of pre-scheduled, automated emails to your leads over a specific period. The goal is to provide valuable content, build trust, and guide your leads through the buyer's journey. By strategically planning and designing these campaigns, you can nurture your leads, increase engagement, and ultimately boost conversion rates.

To begin, it is important to understand the different stages of the buyer's journey and tailor your drip campaigns accordingly. A well-structured drip campaign will consist of emails that are personalized and relevant to each stage, whether it's introducing your brand to new leads or encouraging a purchase from those who are ready to convert.

Segmentation plays a significant role in the success of drip campaigns. By dividing your leads into specific groups based on their interests, behaviors, or demographics, you can deliver highly targeted content that resonates with them. This personalized approach increases the chances of engagement and conversions.

Crafting compelling content is key to a successful drip campaign. Each email in the series should provide value and address the pain points or challenges of your leads. Strive to offer solutions, share educational resources, or provide exclusive discounts and offers. By consistently delivering valuable content, you establish yourself as a trusted authority in your niche, building credibility and fostering long-term relationships.

Automation is a significant advantage of drip campaigns. Utilize an email marketing platform that allows you to schedule and automate the delivery of your emails. This saves time and effort while ensuring that your leads receive timely and relevant messages throughout their journey.

Monitoring and analyzing the performance of your drip campaigns is essential for continuous improvement. Keep track of key metrics such as open rates, click-through rates, and conversions. Analyzing this data will help you identify areas of improvement, optimize your campaigns, and achieve better results over time.

In conclusion, drip campaigns are a powerful tool for nurturing leads in email marketing. By understanding the buyer's journey, segmenting your leads, providing valuable content, and leveraging automation, you can create effective drip campaigns that drive engagement, conversions, and ultimately, business growth.

Utilizing Behavioral Triggers

Utilizing Behavioral Triggers: Unlocking the Power of Email Marketing

In the world of email marketing, the ability to connect with your audience on a personal level is the key to success. No longer can generic mass emails yield the desired results. To truly harness the power of email marketing, you must tap into the psychology of your subscribers. This is where behavioral triggers come into play.

Understanding the concept of behavioral triggers is crucial for anyone delving into the world of email marketing. Behavioral triggers refer to specific actions or behaviors exhibited by your subscribers that can serve as a catalyst for targeted and personalized email campaigns. By capitalizing on these triggers, you can create highly effective campaigns that deliver the right message to the right people at the right time.

One of the most common behavioral triggers is the action of opening an email. When a subscriber takes the time to open your email, it signifies their interest and engagement. This opens up an opportunity for you to provide more tailored content or promotional offers that align with their demonstrated interest. By segmenting your audience based on their open rates, you can create targeted campaigns that will resonate with each group, significantly boosting your conversion rates.

Click-through rates (CTR) are another valuable behavioral trigger to leverage. When a subscriber clicks on a link within your email, it signals a higher level of engagement. This presents an opportunity to send follow-up emails with related content or offers directly related to their click. By doing so, you can provide a seamless journey for your subscribers, leading them down the path to conversion.

Furthermore, utilizing purchase behavior as a behavioral trigger can be highly effective in driving repeat business. By tracking the purchase history of your subscribers, you can send personalized recommendations, exclusive discounts, or complementary products that cater to their specific interests. This not only strengthens the customer relationship but also encourages repeat purchases, ultimately boosting your revenue.

The key to mastering behavioral triggers lies in understanding your audience and their preferences. By constantly analyzing and segmenting your subscriber base, you can identify patterns and behaviors that will allow you to deploy highly targeted and effective email campaigns. By leveraging behavioral triggers, you can build stronger relationships with your subscribers, increase engagement rates, and achieve higher conversion rates.

In conclusion, mastering behavioral triggers is an essential skill for anyone seeking success in email marketing. By understanding the psychology behind subscriber behavior and tailoring your email campaigns accordingly, you can unlock the true potential of email marketing. So, dive into the world of behavioral triggers and watch your email campaigns soar to new heights.

Chapter 7: Segmenting and Targeting Email Campaigns

Importance of Segmentation in Email Marketing

Segmentation is a crucial component of successful email marketing campaigns. It involves dividing your email list into distinct groups based on specific criteria such as demographics, preferences, behavior, or purchase history. By segmenting your audience, you can tailor your email messages to meet the unique needs and interests of each group, resulting in higher engagement rates, increased conversions, and ultimately, better return on investment.

For people who want to learn email marketing, understanding the importance of segmentation is essential. Here's why:

1. Personalization: Segmentation allows you to deliver personalized content to your subscribers. By sending targeted messages that resonate with their individual needs, you can establish a stronger connection and build trust. Personalized emails have a higher chance of being opened, read, and acted upon, leading to higher conversion rates.

2. Increased engagement: When you send relevant content to the right people, you are more likely to capture their attention and keep them engaged. By segmenting your list, you can send emails that are specific to the interests and preferences of each group, increasing the chances of them clicking through, reading, and interacting with your emails.

3. Improved deliverability: Sending emails to a large, unsegmented list can increase the risk of your messages being marked as spam or unsubscribed. However, by segmenting your list, you can ensure that your emails reach the

right people at the right time, reducing the likelihood of spam complaints and improving overall deliverability.

4. Targeted promotions: Segmentation enables you to run targeted promotions and offers, increasing the chances of conversion. By understanding your audience's preferences and purchase history, you can send highly relevant promotions that resonate with their needs, leading to higher click-through rates and more conversions.

5. Better insights and optimization: By analyzing the performance of each segment, you can gain valuable insights into what drives engagement and conversions. This data can help you refine your email marketing strategy, optimize future campaigns, and make data-driven decisions to enhance overall effectiveness.

In conclusion, segmentation plays a vital role in email marketing success. By dividing your audience into specific groups and tailoring your messages accordingly, you can deliver personalized content, increase engagement, improve deliverability, run targeted promotions, and gain valuable insights. As you delve into the world of email marketing, mastering segmentation techniques will significantly enhance the effectiveness of your campaigns and drive better results.

Strategies for Effective Email Segmentation

Email segmentation is a powerful technique that can vastly improve the effectiveness of your email marketing campaigns. By dividing your subscriber list into smaller, more targeted groups, you can deliver personalized and relevant content to each recipient. This not only increases engagement but also boosts conversions and customer loyalty. In this subchapter, we will explore some proven strategies for effective email segmentation to help you master this essential aspect of email marketing.

1. Demographic Segmentation: Start by segmenting your list based on demographic information such as age, gender, location, or job title. This helps you tailor your content to better match the preferences and needs of different groups.

2. Behavioral Segmentation: Analyze your subscribers' behavior, including their past purchases, website interactions, or email engagement. Use this data to segment your list according to specific actions, such as frequent buyers, inactive subscribers, or customers who abandoned their carts. By sending targeted messages based on their behavior, you can re-engage inactive subscribers and drive more conversions.

3. Preference-based Segmentation: Allow your subscribers to self-segment by providing options to choose their preferences, such as content topics, frequency of emails, or preferred communication channels. This empowers your audience and ensures they receive content that aligns with their interests, leading to higher engagement rates.

4. Lifecycle Segmentation: Divide your subscribers based on where they are in the customer journey. For example, new subscribers may receive a welcome series to introduce them to your brand, while loyal customers may receive exclusive offers or rewards. By sending relevant content based on the subscribers' lifecycle stage, you can nurture them effectively and increase their lifetime value.

5. Personalized Segmentation: Utilize personalization techniques to create segments based on individual subscriber data, such as their name, purchase history, or preferences. Personalized emails have been shown to significantly improve open rates, click-through rates, and overall engagement, as they make the recipient feel valued and understood.

Remember, effective email segmentation requires continuous monitoring and analysis of your subscribers' behavior and preferences. Regularly review and update your segments to ensure they remain relevant and effective. By implementing these strategies, you will be able to deliver targeted content that resonates with your audience, resulting in higher engagement, conversions, and long-term success in email marketing.

Mastering email segmentation is crucial for anyone looking to excel in the niche of email marketing. With these strategies at your disposal, you will have the knowledge and tools to create highly effective and personalized email campaigns that deliver remarkable results.

Targeting Specific Customer Segments

In the ever-evolving world of email marketing, reaching the right audience is crucial for achieving success. One-size-fits-all approaches are no longer effective, as consumers expect personalized and tailored experiences. To maximize the impact of your email campaigns, it is essential to identify and target specific customer segments.

Understanding your audience is the first step towards effective segmentation. By analyzing your email list, you can identify common characteristics, preferences, and behaviors. This information will allow you to divide your audience into different segments, enabling you to send more relevant and targeted messages.

Segmentation can be done in various ways, depending on your goals and the nature of your business. Demographic segmentation involves dividing your audience based on variables such as age, gender, location, income, or occupation. This approach is particularly useful for businesses that offer products or services that cater to specific demographics.

Psychographic segmentation, on the other hand, focuses on dividing your audience based on their attitudes, interests, values, and lifestyles. This method helps you understand the motivations and desires of your customers, allowing you to create email campaigns that resonate with their unique preferences.

Behavioral segmentation takes into account the actions and interactions of your audience with your brand. By analyzing their past purchases, browsing history, or engagement with previous email campaigns, you can create segments based on their specific behaviors. This allows you to send targeted emails that promote products or services that align with their interests and needs.

Segmentation not only enhances the relevance of your emails but also improves engagement and conversion rates. When your audience receives emails that address their specific needs and interests, they are more likely to open, read, and click through. This, in turn, increases the chances of generating leads and driving sales.

Moreover, segmentation allows you to implement automation and personalization techniques effectively. By utilizing email marketing tools, you can send automated emails that are triggered by specific actions or events. For example, you can send a personalized welcome email to new subscribers or follow up with customers who have abandoned their shopping carts. These automated emails are highly targeted and can significantly enhance the customer experience.

In conclusion, targeting specific customer segments is a fundamental strategy for mastering email marketing. By understanding your audience and effectively segmenting them based on demographics, psychographics, and behaviors, you can create personalized and relevant email campaigns. This approach improves engagement, increases conversion rates, and enhances overall customer satisfaction. Embrace the power of segmentation, and unlock the true potential of your email marketing campaigns.

Personalization Techniques for Higher Conversions

In the realm of email marketing, personalization is the secret ingredient that can make or break the success of your campaigns. By tailoring your messages to meet the unique needs and preferences of your audience, you can significantly increase engagement and conversions. In this subchapter, we will explore various personalization techniques that have been proven to drive higher conversions in email marketing.

1. Segmenting your audience: One-size-fits-all emails are a thing of the past. To truly connect with your subscribers, you need to segment your audience based on their demographics, interests, and behaviors. By dividing your list into smaller, more targeted segments, you can deliver highly relevant content to each group, increasing the likelihood of conversions.

2. Personalized subject lines: The subject line is the first thing recipients see in their inbox, and it plays a crucial role in determining whether they open your email or not. By incorporating personalization elements such as the recipient's name or location into the subject line, you can grab their attention and pique their curiosity.

3. Dynamic content: Gone are the days of static email content. With dynamic content, you can create personalized email experiences by displaying different sections of your email based on the recipient's preferences or past interactions. For example, you can showcase products similar to those they have previously purchased or highlight promotions specific to their location.

4. Behavior-triggered emails: By leveraging user behavior data, you can send automated emails triggered by specific actions or events. For example, if a subscriber abandons their cart, you can send a personalized reminder email with a discount code to encourage them to complete their purchase. These targeted emails based on user behavior have proven to be highly effective in driving conversions.

5. Personalized recommendations: Utilize the power of data to provide personalized product recommendations to your subscribers. By analyzing their past purchases or browsing history, you can suggest products or services that

align with their interests and preferences. This not only enhances the customer experience but also increases the chances of conversion.

In conclusion, personalization is the key to unlocking higher conversions in email marketing. By segmenting your audience, personalizing subject lines, incorporating dynamic content, utilizing behavior-triggered emails, and offering personalized recommendations, you can create a more tailored and engaging experience for your subscribers. Implementing these techniques will not only boost your conversion rates but also foster stronger relationships with your audience, leading to long-term success in email marketing.

Chapter 8: Measuring Email Marketing Success

Key Metrics for Email Marketing

In the ever-evolving landscape of digital marketing, email marketing remains a powerful tool for businesses to connect with their audience and drive conversions. However, to truly master the art of email marketing, it is crucial to understand and track the key metrics that determine the success of your campaigns. In this subchapter, we will delve into the essential metrics that every email marketer should focus on to optimize their campaigns and achieve desired outcomes.

1. Open Rate: The open rate indicates the percentage of recipients who open your email. It is a fundamental metric that reflects the effectiveness of your subject lines, sender name, and overall email content. A higher open rate signifies a compelling and engaging email, while a low open rate may necessitate reevaluating your approach.

2. Click-through Rate (CTR): The CTR measures the percentage of recipients who clicked on a link within your email. It gauges the level of interest and engagement generated by your email content. A high CTR suggests that your email successfully captured the attention of your audience, compelling them to take further action.

3. Conversion Rate: The conversion rate is a critical metric that measures the percentage of recipients who completed a desired action after clicking through your email. This action could be making a purchase, signing up for a newsletter, or downloading a resource. Tracking your conversion rate helps you assess the effectiveness of your email campaign in achieving your business goals.

4. Bounce Rate: The bounce rate indicates the percentage of emails that were not delivered to recipients' inboxes. A high bounce rate may be caused by invalid or inactive email addresses, technical issues, or stringent spam filters. Monitoring and reducing your bounce rate is essential to maintain a healthy email list and ensure your messages reach the intended recipients.

5. Unsubscribe Rate: The unsubscribe rate represents the percentage of recipients who opted out of receiving future emails from your business. While it is natural to experience some unsubscribes, a consistently high unsubscribe rate should raise concerns about the relevance and value of your email content.

By regularly monitoring and analyzing these key metrics, you can gain valuable insights into the performance of your email marketing campaigns. These metrics enable you to identify areas for improvement, refine your strategies, and ultimately achieve higher engagement, conversions, and return on investment.

Remember, successful email marketing is an ongoing process of experimentation, testing, and optimization. By mastering these key metrics, you will be well-equipped to create effective email campaigns that resonate with your audience and drive your business forward. Stay tuned for the next chapter, where we will explore advanced techniques to enhance your email marketing efforts.

Analyzing Email Campaign Performance

In the world of email marketing, it is not enough to simply send out emails and hope for the best. To truly master email marketing, you need to understand the importance of analyzing your email campaign performance. This subchapter will delve into the essential metrics and strategies to help you evaluate the effectiveness of your email campaigns.

Measuring the success of your email marketing efforts is crucial to improving your campaigns and achieving better results. By analyzing the performance of your campaigns, you can gain valuable insights into what is working and what needs improvement. This data-driven approach will ultimately allow you to make informed decisions and optimize your future campaigns.

One of the key metrics to consider when analyzing your email campaign performance is the open rate. The open rate indicates the percentage of recipients who opened your email. A low open rate may suggest that your subject lines are not compelling enough, or that your emails are ending up in spam folders. By testing different subject lines and email delivery techniques, you can improve your open rates and increase engagement with your audience.

Another important metric to analyze is the click-through rate (CTR). The CTR measures the percentage of recipients who clicked on a link within your email. A high CTR indicates that your email content is engaging and relevant to your audience. By analyzing the click-through rate, you can identify which links and content resonate most with your subscribers, allowing you to tailor your future campaigns accordingly.

Conversion rate is yet another significant metric to track. It measures the percentage of recipients who completed a desired action, such as making a purchase or signing up for a service, after clicking on a link in your email. By analyzing the conversion rate, you can determine the effectiveness of your email campaigns in driving desired outcomes. This analysis will help you optimize your email content, design, and call-to-action elements to improve conversion rates.

Furthermore, it is essential to analyze the unsubscribe rate, bounce rate, and spam complaint rate. These metrics highlight the health of your email list and the overall quality of your campaigns. By closely monitoring these metrics, you can identify potential issues and take corrective actions to maintain a healthy and engaged subscriber base.

In conclusion, analyzing email campaign performance is crucial for anyone looking to master email marketing. By tracking and analyzing key metrics such as open rate, click-through rate, conversion rate, unsubscribe rate, bounce rate, and spam complaint rate, you can gain valuable insights and improve the effectiveness of your campaigns. Remember, email marketing is a continuous learning process, and analyzing campaign performance is an essential part of that journey.

Improving Conversion Rates

In the world of email marketing, the ultimate goal is to drive conversions. After all, what good is a well-crafted email campaign if it doesn't lead to actual results? Fortunately, there are several proven strategies that can help you optimize your conversion rates and achieve the desired outcomes. In this subchapter, we will delve into these strategies and provide you with actionable tips to master the art of improving conversion rates in your email marketing campaigns.

One of the most crucial steps towards improving conversion rates is to segment your email list effectively. By dividing your subscribers into smaller groups based on their interests, demographics, or purchase behavior, you can tailor your email content to resonate with each segment. This personalization increases the chances of subscribers engaging with your emails and taking the desired actions.

Additionally, crafting compelling and attention-grabbing subject lines is paramount. Your subject line is the first impression your subscribers have of your email, so it needs to be enticing enough to compel them to open it. Experimenting with different subject lines, incorporating urgency or curiosity, and A/B testing can help you identify the most effective subject lines for your audience.

Furthermore, optimizing your email content for mobile devices is essential. With the majority of people accessing their emails on smartphones and tablets, your emails must be mobile-friendly. Ensure that your emails have a responsive design, easy-to-read fonts, and clear call-to-action buttons that are easily clickable on smaller screens.

Another effective strategy is to leverage social proof. Including customer testimonials, reviews, or case studies in your emails can instill confidence in your subscribers and encourage them to take the desired action. People are more likely to trust and follow the recommendations of others who have had positive experiences with your brand.

Lastly, regularly analyzing and testing your email campaigns is vital for continuous improvement. Tracking key metrics such as open rates, click-through rates, and conversion rates can provide valuable insights into what is working and what needs adjustment. Experiment with different email layouts, content styles, and calls-to-action to optimize your campaigns over time.

By implementing the strategies discussed in this subchapter, you will be well-equipped to improve your email marketing conversion rates. Remember, email marketing is a dynamic field, so always stay updated with the latest trends, techniques, and industry best practices to ensure the success of your campaigns.

A/B Testing for Optimal Results

A crucial aspect of mastering email marketing lies in understanding the power of A/B testing. This technique allows you to compare two different versions of an email campaign and determine which one yields better results. By systematically testing various elements, you can optimize your email marketing efforts and achieve higher open rates, click-through rates, and ultimately, better campaign performance.

Why is A/B testing important in email marketing? It provides valuable insights into what resonates with your audience, allowing you to make data-driven decisions rather than relying on guesswork. By testing different variations of subject lines, email design, call-to-action buttons, layouts, or even the timing of your campaigns, you can identify the most effective strategies for engaging your subscribers.

To conduct an A/B test, begin by selecting one element of your email campaign to test. This could be the subject line, content, visuals, or any other variable you believe could impact the success of your campaign. Split your email list into two groups: group A and group B. Send version A of your email to group A and version B to group B, ensuring that only one variable is different between the two versions.

Now, closely monitor the performance metrics of each version. Pay attention to open rates, click-through rates, conversions, and any other relevant data. After a sufficient amount of time, analyze the results to determine which version performs better. This winning version should then become the benchmark for future campaigns, while you continue testing other variables to further optimize your strategies.

Remember, A/B testing is an ongoing process. As consumer preferences evolve, so should your email marketing tactics. Continuously test and refine different elements to ensure your campaigns remain effective and relevant. Some elements you may consider testing include personalized subject lines, different email lengths, different images or fonts, or even different sender names.

In conclusion, A/B testing is a powerful tool for optimizing your email marketing campaigns. By systematically testing various elements and analyzing the results, you can gain valuable insights into your audience's preferences and tailor your campaigns accordingly. Remember to focus on one variable at a time and use the winning version as your benchmark for future campaigns. Stay up to date with the latest trends and continuously test and refine your strategies to achieve optimal results in your email marketing efforts.

Chapter 9

Enhancing Email Marketing with Advanced Strategies

Incorporating Social Media into Email Campaigns

As email marketing continues to evolve, it has become increasingly important for businesses to integrate social media into their email campaigns. With the rise of social media platforms like Facebook, Twitter, and Instagram, it is crucial for email marketers to leverage these channels to reach a wider audience and enhance their overall marketing efforts. In this subchapter, we will explore the benefits of incorporating social media into email campaigns and provide practical strategies for effective integration.

One of the primary advantages of incorporating social media into email campaigns is the ability to expand your reach. By sharing your email content on social media platforms, you can engage with a larger audience and attract new subscribers who may not be familiar with your brand. Additionally, social media enables your subscribers to easily share your email content with their networks, increasing the potential for viral marketing and exponential growth.

Another benefit of integrating social media into email campaigns is the opportunity for cross-promotion. By including social media icons and links in your emails, you can encourage your subscribers to follow your brand on social media. This allows you to build a stronger online presence and foster ongoing engagement with your audience. Furthermore, by promoting your email campaigns on social media, you can generate anticipation and excitement, leading to higher open and click-through rates.

To effectively incorporate social media into email campaigns, it is important to align your messaging and branding across all channels. Consistency in tone, visuals, and content helps to establish a cohesive brand image and enhance brand recognition. Additionally, integrating user-generated content from social media into your email campaigns can build trust and authenticity, as it showcases real customer experiences and testimonials.

In terms of practical strategies, consider using social media to conduct polls or surveys to gather insights and preferences from your audience. This data can then be used to personalize your email campaigns and deliver more relevant content. Additionally, leverage social media influencers or brand advocates to amplify your email campaigns and reach a wider audience. Collaborating with influencers who align with your brand values can help you tap into their loyal following and increase the credibility of your email campaigns.

In conclusion, incorporating social media into email campaigns is a valuable strategy that can significantly enhance your email marketing efforts. By expanding your reach, promoting cross-engagement, and aligning your messaging and branding, you can create a powerful synergy between email and social media platforms. By adopting these strategies, you will be able to master the art of email marketing and achieve more effective and successful campaigns.

Integrating Email with Other Marketing Channels

In today's digital landscape, successful marketing campaigns require a multi-channel approach. Email marketing, while highly effective on its own, can be further enhanced by integrating it with other marketing channels. By combining the power of email with various platforms and strategies, you can create a cohesive and impactful marketing campaign that reaches a wider audience and drives better results.

Social media is one of the most prominent channels that can be integrated with email marketing. By incorporating social sharing buttons in your emails, you can encourage recipients to share your content on their social networks. This not only expands your reach but also increases the chances of your emails being seen by new potential customers. Additionally, you can use social media to promote your email campaigns, enticing followers to subscribe and stay updated with your latest offers and content.

Content marketing is another valuable channel to integrate with email marketing. By creating informative and engaging content, such as blog posts, videos, or whitepapers, you can attract a larger audience and establish your brand as an industry authority. Email can then be used to distribute this valuable content to your subscribers, ensuring that they stay engaged and informed. Furthermore, by including links to your content in your emails, you can drive traffic to your website or landing pages, increasing conversions and nurturing leads.

Another powerful integration is with customer relationship management (CRM) systems. By syncing your email marketing platform with your CRM, you can effectively track and manage customer interactions across different channels. This allows you to personalize your email campaigns based on customer preferences and behaviors, resulting in higher engagement and conversion rates. Moreover, integrating email with CRM enables you to automate various marketing processes, such as lead nurturing and customer segmentation, saving you time and effort.

Lastly, integrating email marketing with mobile marketing is crucial in today's mobile-first world. With the majority of emails being opened on mobile devices, it is essential to optimize your emails for mobile viewing. Additionally, you can leverage SMS marketing to complement your email campaigns, delivering time-sensitive offers or important updates directly to your subscribers' mobile phones.

In conclusion, by integrating email with other marketing channels, you can amplify the reach and impact of your campaigns. Whether it's social media, content marketing, CRM, or mobile marketing, each integration brings unique benefits that contribute to a holistic and effective email marketing strategy. Embrace the power of integration and unlock the full potential of your email campaigns.

Leveraging User-Generated Content

In today's digital age, user-generated content has emerged as a powerful tool for marketers seeking to engage and connect with their audience. Email marketing, in particular, can greatly benefit from leveraging user-generated content to create more effective campaigns. By harnessing the creativity, authenticity, and enthusiasm of your customers, you can enhance the impact of your email marketing initiatives and foster stronger relationships with your audience.

User-generated content refers to any type of content that is created and shared by individuals who are not professionally affiliated with a brand. This can include customer reviews, testimonials, social media posts, images, videos, and more. The key advantage of user-generated content is its ability to build trust and credibility. When people see their peers sharing positive experiences with a brand, they are more likely to trust and engage with that brand themselves.

In the context of email marketing, user-generated content can be leveraged in various ways. One effective strategy is to include customer testimonials or reviews in your email campaigns. By featuring real stories and experiences from satisfied customers, you can provide social proof to your subscribers, encouraging them to take action and make a purchase.

Another way to leverage user-generated content is by running contests or campaigns that encourage customers to share their own content related to your brand. This can be done through social media platforms or dedicated landing pages. By offering incentives or rewards for participation, you can generate a wealth of user-generated content that can be repurposed in your email campaigns. This not only adds a personal touch to your emails but also allows you to showcase your customers and their experiences, making them feel valued and appreciated.

Furthermore, user-generated content can also be utilized to create dynamic and engaging email content. Incorporating real customer images or videos into your emails can significantly enhance their visual appeal and capture the attention of your subscribers. This can be particularly effective for industries such as travel, fashion, or food, where visual content plays a crucial role in decision-making.

To effectively leverage user-generated content in your email marketing campaigns, it is important to establish clear guidelines and permissions for using customer-generated content. Always seek permission from the content creators and give them proper credit for their contributions. Additionally, ensure that the content aligns with your brand values and messaging to maintain consistency and authenticity.

In conclusion, user-generated content is a powerful asset for email marketers looking to connect with their audience on a deeper level. By incorporating real experiences, testimonials, and visuals created by your customers, you can build trust, engage your subscribers, and create more impactful email campaigns. Embracing user-generated content allows you to tap into the collective creativity and passion of your audience, fostering a sense of community and loyalty around your brand.

Retargeting and Remarketing Techniques

In the fast-paced world of email marketing, it is crucial to stay ahead of the competition and engage with your audience effectively. One powerful strategy that can significantly impact the success of your email campaigns is the use of retargeting and remarketing techniques. These techniques allow you to re-engage with users who have shown interest in your brand or products, increasing the chances of conversion and fostering long-term customer relationships.

Retargeting involves displaying targeted ads to users who have visited your website or interacted with your emails but did not convert. By placing a small piece of code, known as a pixel, on your website, you can track these users and show them relevant ads across various platforms, such as social media or other websites they visit. This ensures that your brand stays top of mind and encourages them to revisit your website and complete the desired action.

Remarketing, on the other hand, focuses on re-engaging with users who have already subscribed to your email list. It involves creating personalized email campaigns based on the user's previous interactions with your brand, such as their purchase history or browsing behavior. By tailoring your content to their specific interests and needs, you can deliver highly relevant and engaging emails, increasing the likelihood of conversions and customer loyalty.

To effectively implement retargeting and remarketing techniques, it is essential to segment your audience based on their behavior and preferences. By analyzing their past interactions, you can create specific segments and develop targeted campaigns that resonate with each group. This allows you to deliver personalized content, offers, and recommendations, maximizing the chances of conversion and customer satisfaction.

Furthermore, it is crucial to constantly monitor and optimize your retargeting and remarketing campaigns. Analyze the performance metrics, such as click-through rates, conversion rates, and return on ad spend, to understand the effectiveness of your efforts. Test different ad formats, messaging, and targeting options to find the most successful combinations for your audience.

By mastering retargeting and remarketing techniques, you can leverage the power of email marketing to its fullest potential. Engaging with users who have already shown interest in your brand or products can significantly increase conversions, customer loyalty, and ultimately, the success of your email campaigns. Stay ahead of the competition and build lasting relationships with your audience through effective retargeting and remarketing strategies.

Chapter 10

Best Practices and Future Trends in Email Marketing

Staying Compliant with Email Marketing Regulations

In the ever-evolving landscape of email marketing, it is crucial for marketers to stay up to date with the latest regulations to ensure their campaigns remain effective and legal. Email marketing regulations are in place to protect consumers from spam and unwanted communications, and failing to comply with these regulations can result in severe consequences, including legal penalties and damage to your brand's reputation. This subchapter aims to provide you with a comprehensive understanding of the regulations governing email marketing and equip you with the knowledge and strategies to stay compliant.

First and foremost, it is essential to familiarize yourself with the key regulations that govern email marketing. The most prominent legislation is the CAN-SPAM Act, which stands for Controlling the Assault of Non-Solicited Pornography and Marketing. This Act sets forth strict guidelines for commercial email messages, including requirements for opt-out mechanisms, accurate header information, and clear identification of the message as an advertisement.

To comply with the CAN-SPAM Act, it is crucial to obtain explicit permission from recipients before sending them marketing emails. Building a permission-based email list ensures that your contacts have willingly opted in to receive communications from your brand, reducing the risk of complaints and potential legal issues. Additionally, providing a clear and easily accessible unsubscribe option in every email allows recipients to opt out at any time, as mandated by the Act.

Another significant regulation to consider is the General Data Protection Regulation (GDPR), which applies to marketers targeting individuals within the European Union (EU). The GDPR focuses on data protection and privacy, requiring explicit consent for collecting and processing personal data. It is essential to understand the GDPR's requirements, such as providing transparent information about data collection and usage, obtaining consent separately for different processing purposes, and ensuring data security.

Beyond specific regulations, it is advisable to adopt best practices for email marketing compliance. Regularly reviewing and updating your email lists to remove inactive or disengaged subscribers helps maintain a healthy sender reputation and ensures your messages reach the intended audience. Implementing a double opt-in process, where subscribers confirm their email address and consent, provides an additional layer of protection against potential complaints.

In conclusion, staying compliant with email marketing regulations is not only essential for legal reasons but also for maintaining a positive brand image and building trust with your audience. By understanding and adhering to regulations like the CAN-SPAM Act and GDPR, as well as implementing best practices, you can create effective and ethical email marketing campaigns that resonate with your subscribers and drive desired results.

Managing Subscriber Preferences and Opt-outs

In the world of email marketing, building and maintaining a strong subscriber base is crucial for the success of any campaign. However, it is equally important to respect the preferences of your subscribers and provide them with the option to opt-out if they no longer wish to receive your emails. This subchapter will delve into the significance of managing subscriber preferences and opt-outs and provide proven strategies to ensure effective email campaigns.

Understanding subscriber preferences is the first step towards creating a personalized and engaging email experience. By allowing subscribers to choose their preferences such as the frequency of emails, content topics, or preferred communication channels, you can tailor your campaigns to meet their individual needs. This not only enhances the subscriber experience but also boosts engagement and conversions.

To effectively manage subscriber preferences, it is essential to implement a robust email marketing platform that offers advanced segmentation and automation capabilities. These tools enable you to categorize subscribers based on their preferences and send targeted emails that align with their interests. By providing relevant content, you increase the chances of subscribers staying engaged and less likely to opt-out.

Opt-outs are an inevitable part of email marketing, and it is crucial to handle them gracefully. Make the opt-out process simple and easy for subscribers by including a prominent unsubscribe link in your emails. This not only complies with anti-spam regulations but also helps build trust and credibility with your audience. Remember, it is better to have a smaller engaged subscriber list than a larger one filled with disinterested recipients.

Regularly monitoring and analyzing opt-out rates can provide valuable insights into the effectiveness of your email campaigns. High opt-out rates may indicate a need for improvement in content relevance, frequency, or overall strategy. By constantly evaluating and adjusting your campaigns based on subscriber feedback, you can minimize opt-outs and maximize engagement.

Lastly, always honor opt-out requests promptly. Failing to remove unsubscribed individuals from your email list not only damages your reputation but also violates privacy regulations. Ensure that your email marketing platform automatically updates unsubscribed contacts and suppresses them from future campaigns.

In conclusion, managing subscriber preferences and opt-outs is vital for successful email marketing campaigns. By respecting your subscribers' preferences, providing personalized content, and simplifying the opt-out process, you can foster trust, enhance engagement, and maintain a healthy subscriber base. Remember, effective email marketing is about quality, not just quantity.

Adapting to Evolving Email Marketing Trends

In the ever-changing landscape of digital marketing, one aspect has remained constant - the power of email marketing. Email has proven to be a highly effective tool for businesses to connect with their audience, generate leads, and drive conversions. However, with the rapid advancement of technology and changing consumer behaviors, it is essential for email marketers to stay ahead of the curve and adapt to evolving trends.

This subchapter aims to provide valuable insights and strategies for individuals who want to learn email marketing and stay at the forefront of the industry. By embracing and implementing these trends, email marketers can maximize the effectiveness of their campaigns and achieve remarkable results.

One of the key trends in email marketing is personalization. Gone are the days of generic mass emails. Today, consumers expect a tailored experience. By utilizing data and segmentation techniques, marketers can create personalized emails that resonate with their audience, increasing engagement and conversions.

Another significant trend is the rise of mobile email. With the increasing use of smartphones and tablets, it is crucial for email marketers to optimize their campaigns for mobile devices. Responsive design, concise and scannable content, and clear call-to-action buttons are some of the best practices to ensure a seamless mobile experience for recipients.

Automation is yet another trend that has revolutionized email marketing. By leveraging automation tools and workflows, marketers can send timely and relevant emails based on customer behavior and preferences. From welcome emails to cart abandonment reminders, automation can significantly improve the efficiency and effectiveness of email campaigns.

Furthermore, integrating social media into email marketing is becoming increasingly important. By including social sharing buttons and encouraging recipients to engage with the brand on social platforms, marketers can extend the reach of their emails and foster a sense of community.

Lastly, the growing concern for data privacy and security cannot be ignored. With regulations like GDPR and CCPA in place, email marketers must ensure compliance and gain the trust of their subscribers by being transparent about data usage and providing options to manage preferences.

In conclusion, email marketing continues to be a powerful tool for businesses, but to be successful, marketers must adapt to evolving trends. By embracing personalization, optimizing for mobile, leveraging automation, integrating social media, and prioritizing data privacy, email marketers can stay ahead of the game and achieve remarkable results.

Innovations and Predictions for the Future of Email Marketing

Email marketing has long been a staple in the world of digital marketing. It has proven to be a highly effective tool for businesses to connect with their audience, build relationships, and drive sales. However, as technology continues to evolve, so does the email marketing landscape. In this subchapter, we will explore the innovations and predictions that are shaping the future of email marketing.

One of the most significant innovations in email marketing is the rise of automation and personalization. With advancements in AI and machine learning, marketers can now create highly targeted and personalized email campaigns. By analyzing customer data and behavior, emails can be sent at the right time, with the right content, and to the right audience. This level of personalization not only increases engagement but also improves the overall customer experience.

Another innovation that is gaining traction is interactive emails. Traditionally, emails have been static and one-directional. However, interactive elements such as quizzes, polls, and sliders can now be embedded directly into emails. This not only makes emails more engaging but also allows marketers to gather valuable data and insights from their audience.

The future of email marketing also lies in mobile optimization. With the majority of people now accessing their emails on mobile devices, it is crucial for marketers to ensure that their emails are mobile-friendly. Responsive design, concise content, and clear call-to-action buttons are some of the key elements that will help optimize emails for mobile users.

Predictions for the future of email marketing include the integration of artificial intelligence and voice-activated assistants. AI-powered email marketing platforms will be able to analyze vast amounts of data, predict consumer behavior, and automate email campaigns with minimal human intervention. Moreover, as voice-activated assistants like Siri and Alexa become more prevalent, marketers will need to optimize their emails for voice search.

In conclusion, the future of email marketing holds exciting innovations and predictions. Automation and personalization, interactive emails, mobile optimization, and the integration of AI and voice-activated assistants are just some of the trends that will shape the email marketing landscape. As a marketer, it is crucial to stay up-to-date with these advancements and adapt your email marketing strategies accordingly to stay ahead of the competition and achieve maximum engagement and conversions.

Appendix:

Email Marketing Glossary

In the realm of email marketing, a plethora of terms and acronyms are used that might initially seem daunting to beginners. To assist you in navigating this digital landscape, we have compiled an email marketing glossary that will demystify the jargon and empower you to embark on effective email campaigns. Whether you are a novice or an experienced marketer, this glossary will serve as a valuable reference tool.

1. Autoresponder: An automated email campaign that is triggered by a specific action or event, such as a new subscriber signing up for your newsletter.

2. Bounce Rate: The percentage of emails that were not successfully delivered to recipients due to various reasons, like invalid or inactive email addresses.

3. Call to Action (CTA): A prompt within an email that encourages readers to take a specific action, such as making a purchase or signing up for a webinar.

4. Conversion Rate: The percentage of recipients who complete the desired action, such as making a purchase or filling out a form, after receiving an email.

5. Drip Campaign: A series of pre-scheduled emails sent to subscribers over a specific period, designed to nurture leads and guide them through the sales funnel.

6. KPI (Key Performance Indicator): Quantifiable metrics used to evaluate the success of an email campaign, such as open rate, click-through rate, and conversion rate.

7. List Segmentation: Dividing your email list into smaller, targeted groups based on specific criteria such as demographics, interests, or purchase history, to personalize and optimize your email campaigns.

8. Open Rate: The percentage of recipients who open an email, indicating the effectiveness of subject lines and sender reputation.

9. Personalization: Tailoring email content to individual recipients based on their preferences, demographics, or behavior, to create a more personalized and engaging experience.

10. Spam Score: A numerical rating that indicates the likelihood of an email being classified as spam, based on various factors such as email content, sender reputation, and email structure.

11. Unsubscribe Rate: The percentage of recipients who choose to opt-out or unsubscribe from your email list, often influenced by factors like email frequency or irrelevant content.

By familiarizing yourself with these key terms, you will gain a solid foundation in email marketing, enabling you to plan, execute, and optimize effective email campaigns. Remember, email marketing is a dynamic field that continually evolves, so staying updated on the latest trends and practices is crucial. With this glossary at your disposal, you can confidently navigate the intricacies of email marketing and propel your campaigns towards success.

Mastering Email Marketing: Proven Strategies for Effective Campaigns is the perfect resource for people who want to learn email marketing. Packed with practical tips, industry insights, and real-life examples, this book will equip you with the knowledge and skills necessary to create compelling email campaigns that engage subscribers, drive conversions, and yield impressive results. Whether you are a small business owner, marketer, or aspiring email marketer, this book will guide you through the intricacies of email marketing, helping you unlock its full potential.

Recommended Tools and Resources

When it comes to mastering email marketing, having the right tools and resources at your disposal can make a world of difference. In this subchapter, we will explore some of the top tools and resources that are highly recommended for people who want to learn email marketing and are specifically interested in the niche of email marketing.

1. Email Service Providers (ESPs): One of the most crucial tools for any email marketer is an ESP. These platforms enable you to manage your email campaigns, create visually appealing templates, segment your audience, and track the performance of your campaigns. Some popular ESPs include Mailchimp, Constant Contact, and Campaign Monitor.

2. Automation Software: Email automation is a game-changer in the world of email marketing. It allows you to set up automated email sequences based on triggers or user actions. Tools like ActiveCampaign, ConvertKit, and Drip offer powerful automation features that can save you time and help you deliver personalized and timely content to your subscribers.

3. Email Analytics and Reporting: To measure the success of your email campaigns, you need access to accurate and detailed analytics. Tools like Google Analytics, Litmus, and Email on Acid provide insights into open rates, click-through rates, conversion rates, and other important metrics. These tools help you understand what works and what doesn't, allowing you to optimize your strategies accordingly.

4. Email Validations and Verifications: Maintaining a clean and healthy email list is essential for successful email marketing. Email validation and verification tools like NeverBounce, ZeroBounce, and BriteVerify help you remove invalid or inactive email addresses from your list, ensuring that your emails reach the right audience and improving your deliverability rates.

5. Email Design and Testing: Creating visually appealing and mobile-friendly email templates is crucial for engaging your subscribers. Tools like Litmus, Mailtrap, and EmailReach provide comprehensive testing and rendering capabilities, allowing you to preview your emails across different devices and email clients, ensuring they appear as intended.

6. Email Marketing Blogs and Communities: Staying up-to-date with the latest trends, strategies, and best practices is vital for email marketers. Following industry-leading blogs, such as Email Marketing Daily, Email on Acid's Blog, and Litmus Blog, can help you stay informed and provide valuable insights. Engaging with email marketing communities like the Email Marketing Forum and Email Geeks Slack Community also allows you to network with like-minded professionals and learn from their experiences.

These recommended tools and resources are just the tip of the iceberg in the world of email marketing. By leveraging these tools and staying updated with the latest trends and strategies, you can take your email marketing campaigns to new heights and achieve remarkable results.

Sample Email Templates

In today's digital age, email marketing has become an essential tool for businesses of all sizes. It allows you to connect with your audience, build relationships, and drive conversions. However, crafting compelling and effective emails can be a daunting task, especially for beginners in the field of email marketing. That's why we have compiled a collection of sample email templates to help you get started on your email marketing journey.

1. Welcome Email Template:
Subject: Welcome to [Your Company Name]!

Dear [Subscriber's Name],

We are thrilled to have you join our community at [Your Company Name]. As a valued subscriber, you will now have access to exclusive updates, offers, and information. We look forward to delivering exciting content straight to your inbox.

In the meantime, we encourage you to explore our website and learn more about our products/services. If you have any questions or need assistance, feel free to reach out to our support team.

Thank you once again for joining us. We can't wait to embark on this journey together!

Best regards,
[Your Name]
[Your Company Name]

2. Product Announcement Template:
Subject: Introducing [New Product/Service] - Elevate Your [Problem]

Hello [Subscriber's Name],

We are excited to introduce our latest offering - [New Product/Service]. Say goodbye to [Problem] and hello to a world of possibilities. Our new solution is designed to [highlight key benefits]. Here's a quick glimpse of what you can expect:

- Benefit 1: [Description]
- Benefit 2: [Description]
- Benefit 3: [Description]

To learn more about how [New Product/Service] can transform your life, visit our website or contact our sales team for a personalized demo.

Don't miss out on this game-changing opportunity. Get ahead of the competition and unlock your full potential with [New Product/Service] today!

Best regards,
[Your Name]
[Your Company Name]

3. Abandoned Cart Reminder Template:
Subject: Don't Forget About Your [Product/Service]!

Hello [Subscriber's Name],

We noticed that you recently added [Product/Service] to your cart but haven't completed your purchase yet. We understand that life can get busy, so we wanted to send you a friendly reminder.

Remember, [Product/Service] is waiting for you! Here are a few reasons why you should complete your purchase:

- Reason 1: [Description]
- Reason 2: [Description]
- Reason 3: [Description]

To complete your purchase, simply click the link below or head over to our website. If you have any questions or concerns, our support team is here to assist you.

Thank you for considering [Your Company Name]. We hope to see you soon!

Best regards,
[Your Name]
[Your Company Name]

These sample email templates are just a starting point. Feel free to customize them to align with your brand voice and goals. Remember, successful email marketing is all about delivering value to your subscribers and building meaningful connections. Good luck on your email marketing journey!

www.ingramcontent.com/pod-product-compliance
Lightning Source LLC
Chambersburg PA
CBHW062243290526
45794CB00006B/2390